Coloring book

Vol.1

summer

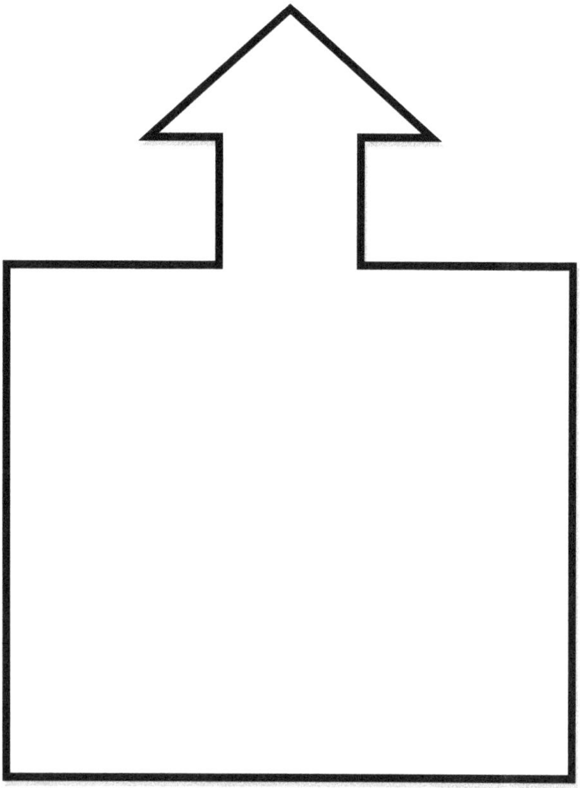

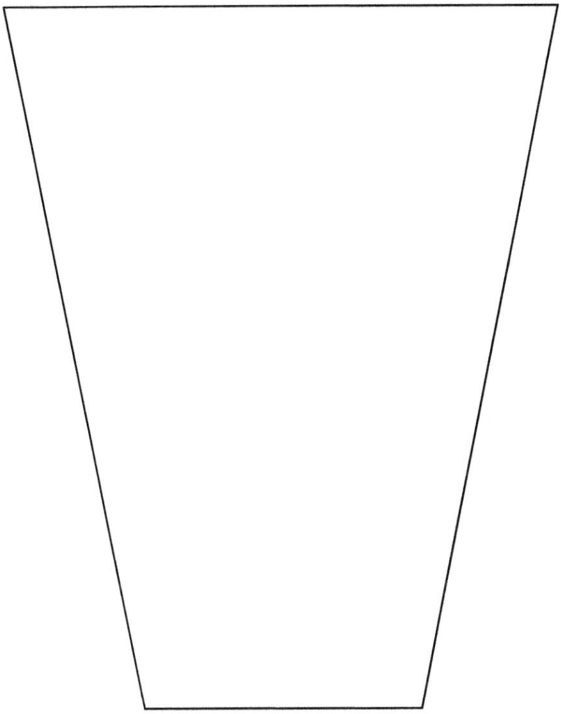

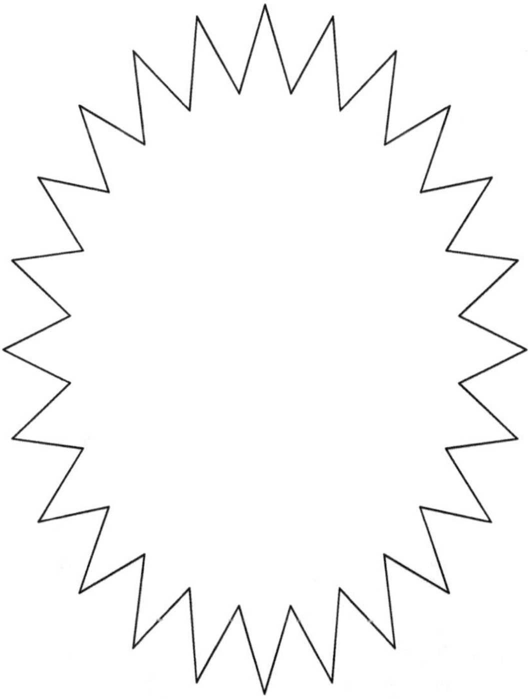

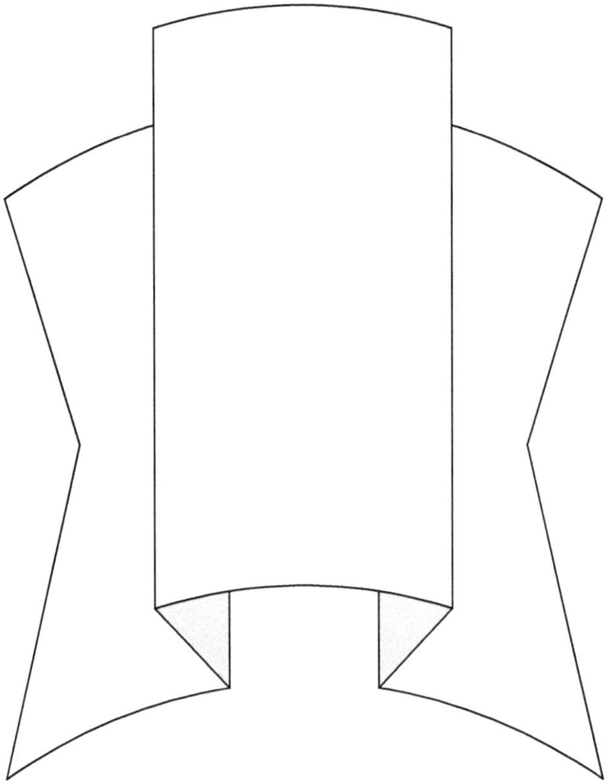

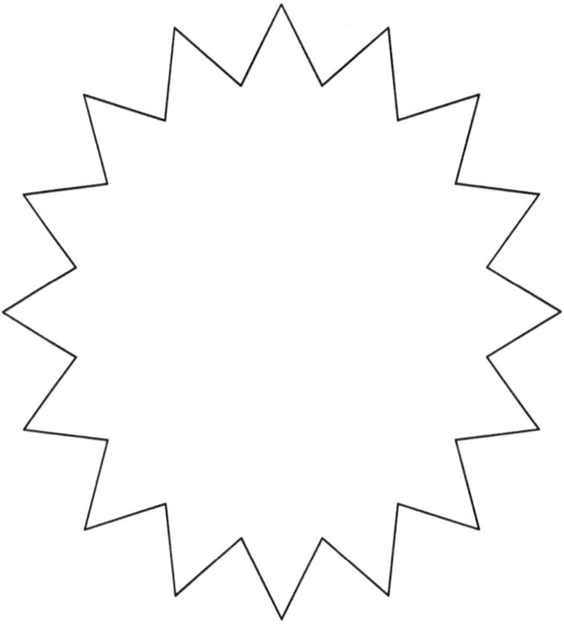

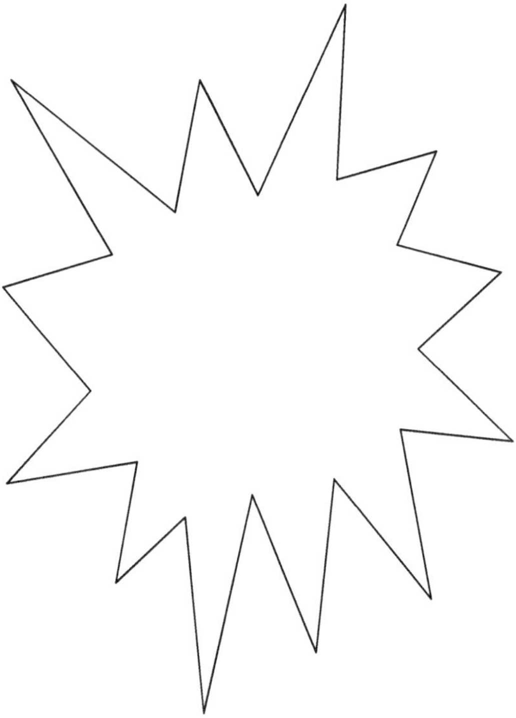

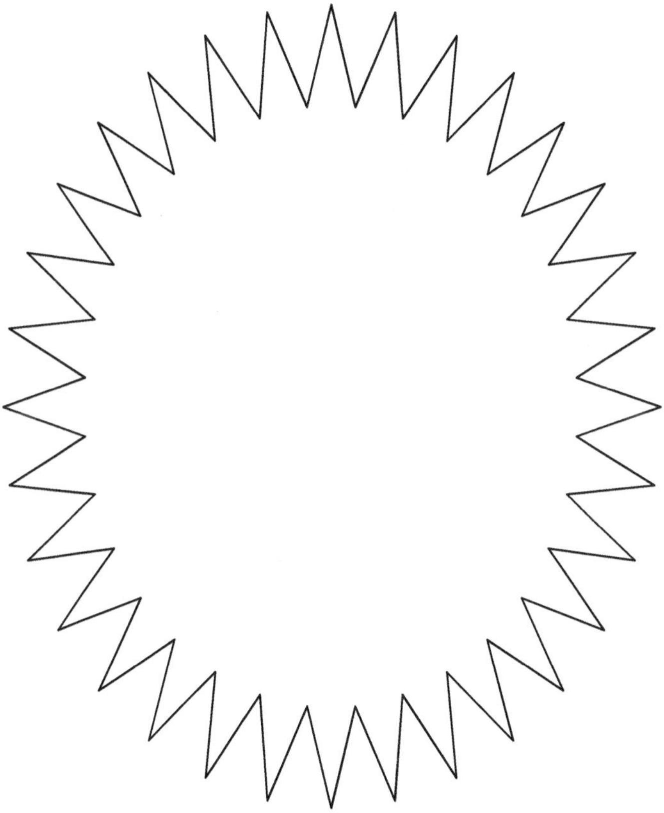

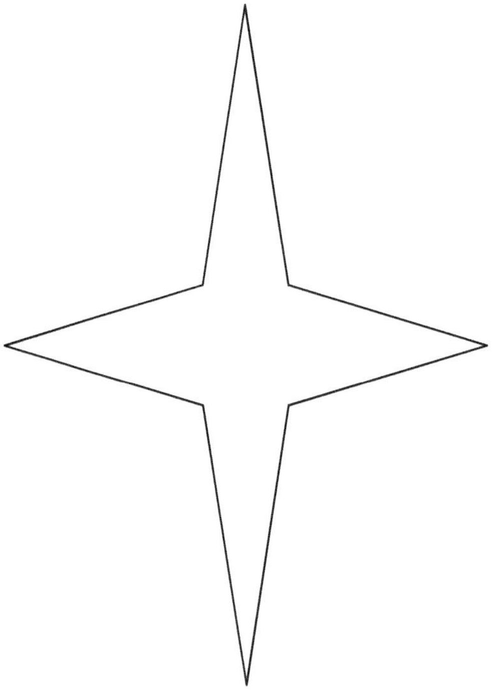

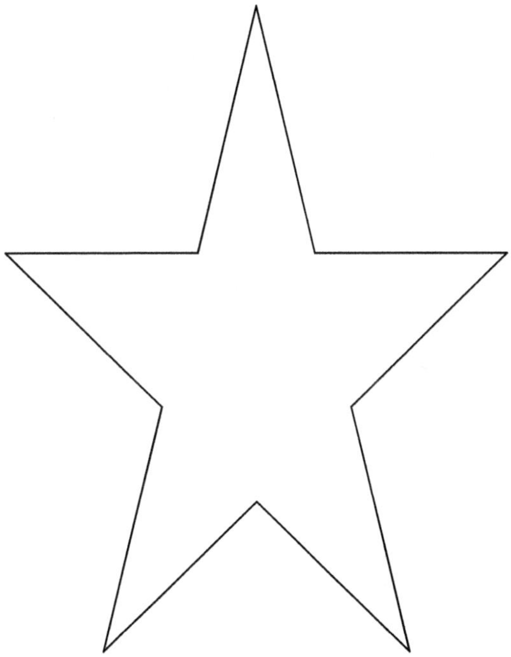

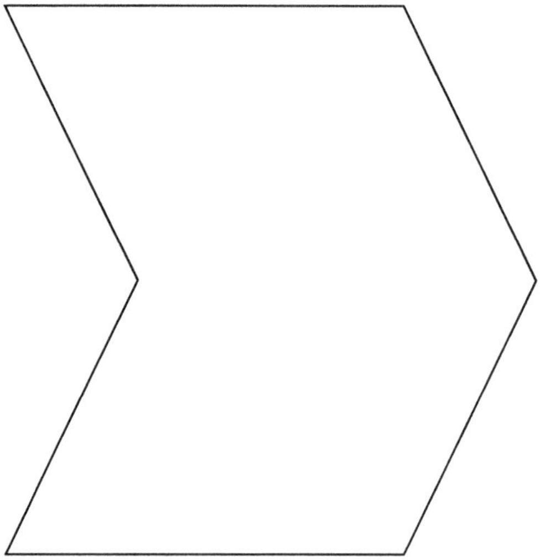

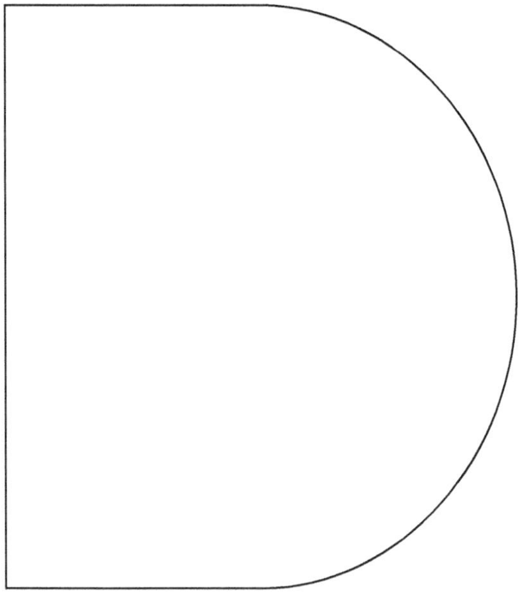

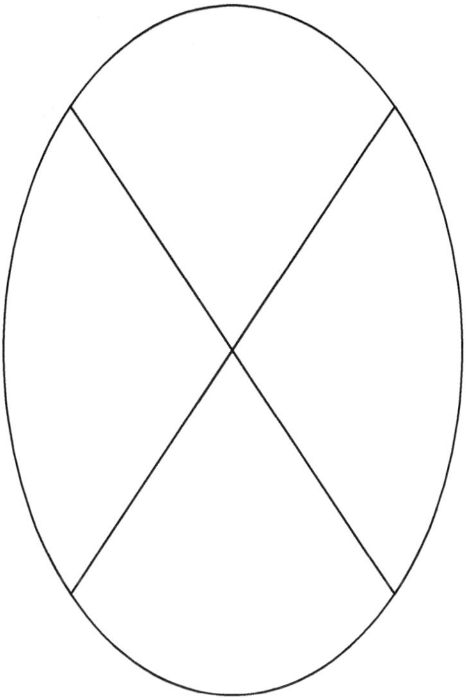

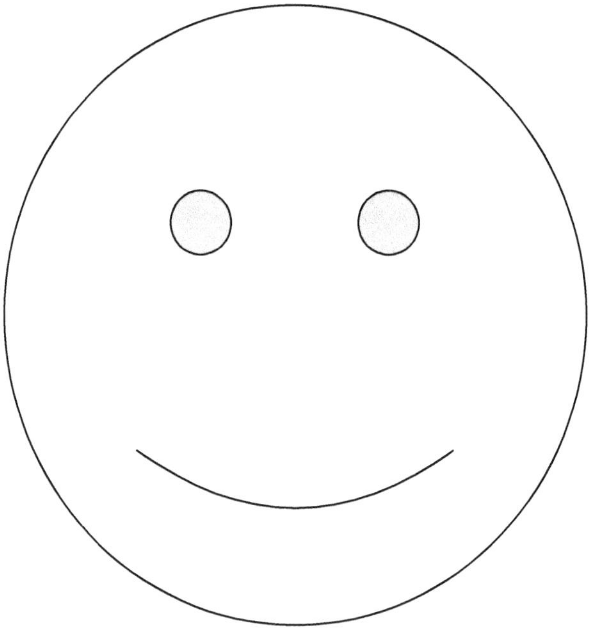

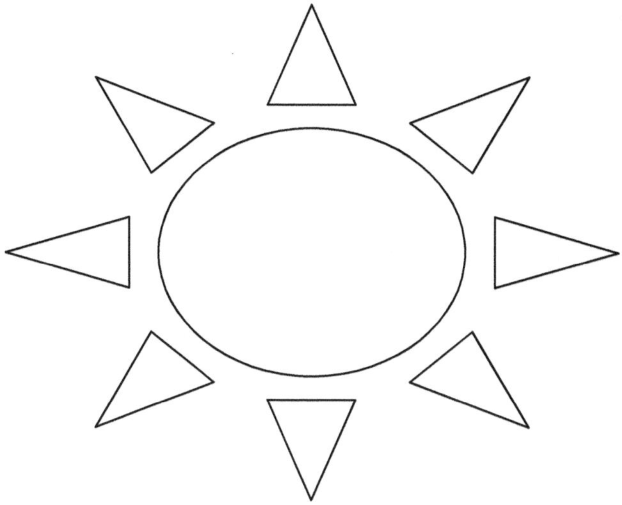

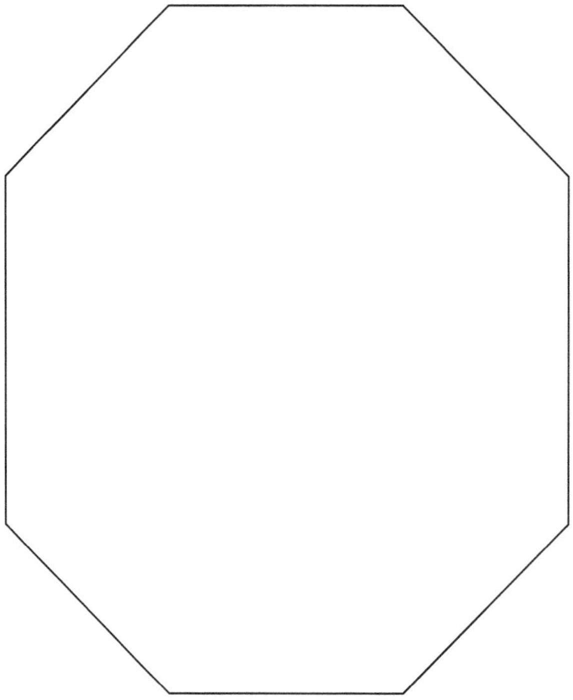

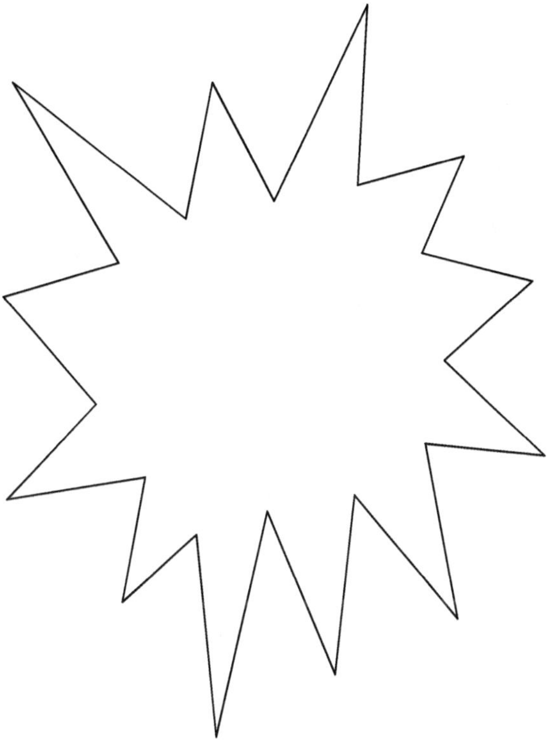

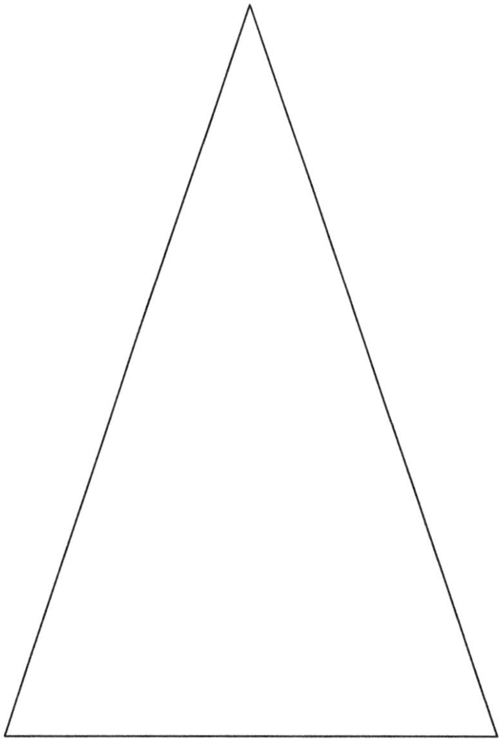

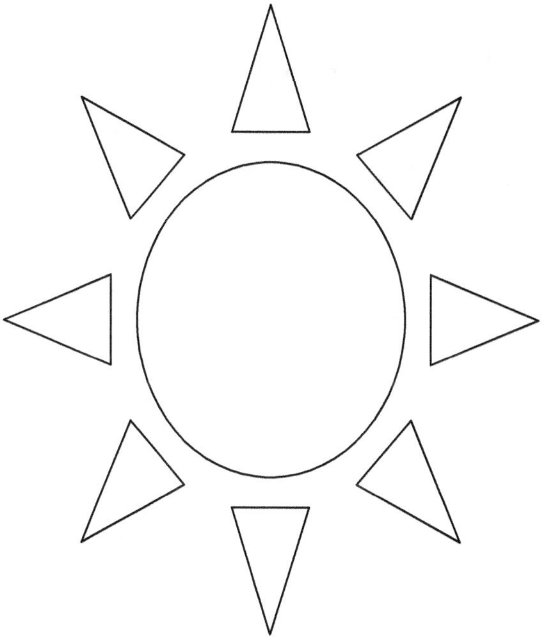

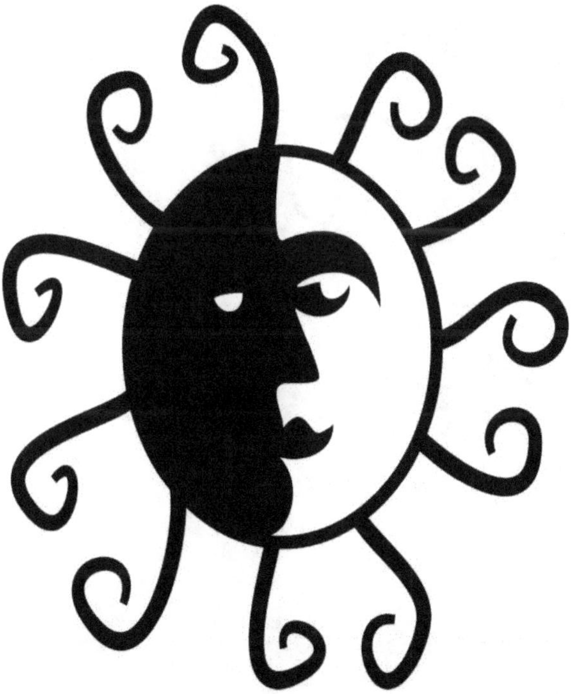

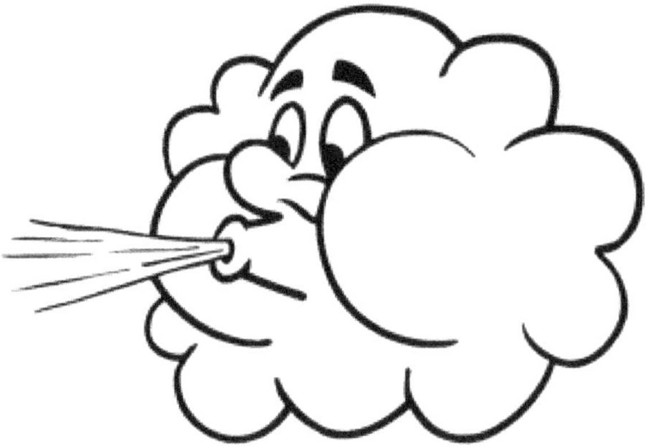

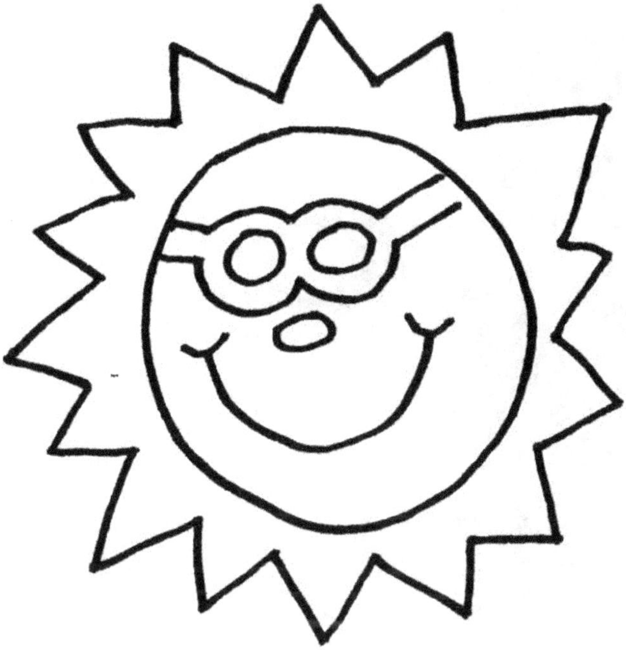

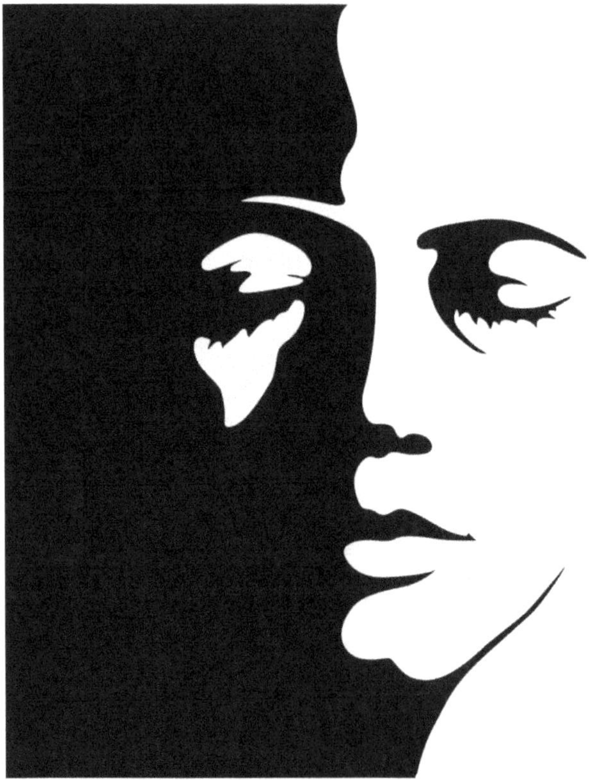

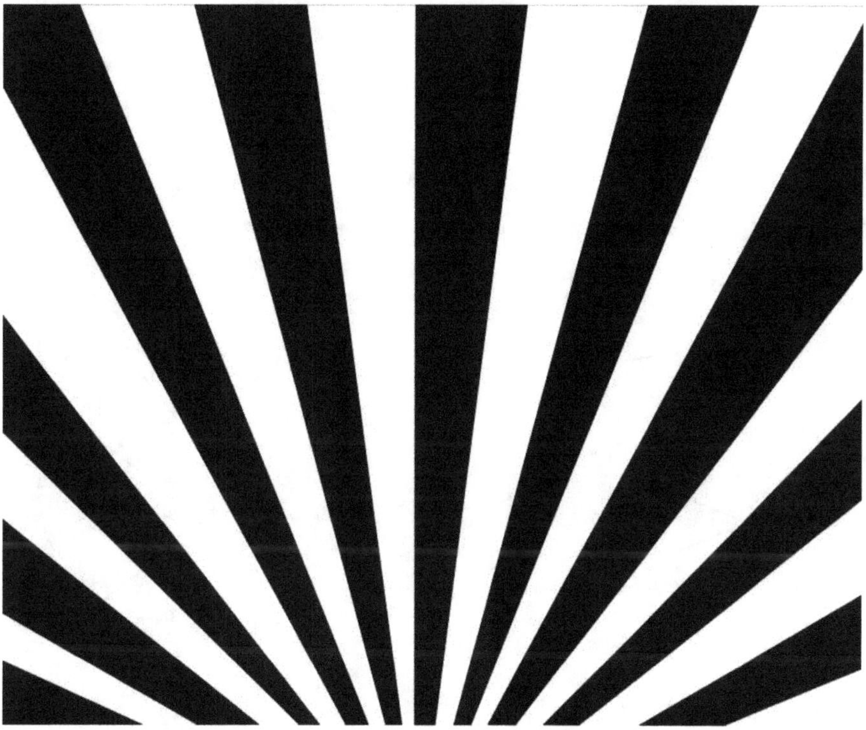

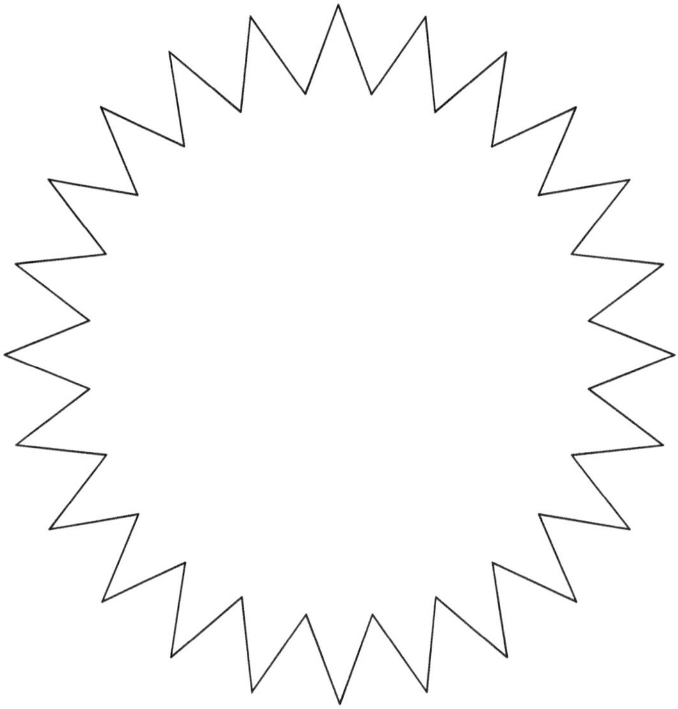

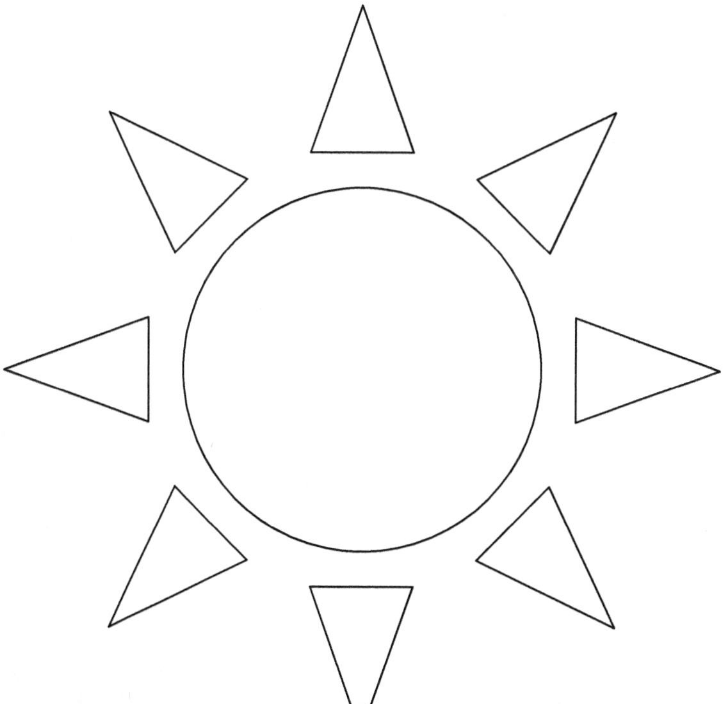

www.ingramcontent.com/pod-product-compliance
Lightning Source LLC
Chambersburg PA
CBHW070927180526
45168CB00005B/2180
9781511827898